Nobel Prize medal for Literature.

Certificate of Nobel Prize for Literature.

Kawabata's speech

King Gustav Adolf presents the Nobel Prize to Kawabata

Yasunari Kawabata

YASUNARI KAWABATA

JAPAN
THE BEAUTIFUL
AND MYSELF

The 1968 Nobel Prize acceptance speech with the English translation by Edward G. Seidensticker

KODANSHA INTERNATIONAL LTD.
TOKYO AND PALO ALTO

Published by Kodansha International Ltd., 2-12-21;
Otowa, Bunkyo-ku, Tokyo, Japan and Kodansha
International/USA, Ltd., 599 College Avenue, Palo
Alto, California 94306. Copyright, 1968, the Nobel
Foundation. All rights reserved. Printed in Japan.
LCC 75-90028
SBN 87011-088-8
JBC No. 1295-781057-2361

First edition, 1969
Second printing, 1971

*"In the spring, cherry blossoms,
in the summer the cuckoo.
In autumn the moon, and in
winter the snow, clear, cold."*

*"Winter moon, coming from the
clouds to keep me company,
Is the wind piercing, the snow cold?"*

The first of these poems is by the priest Dōgen (1200–1253) and bears the title "Innate Spirit." The second is by the priest Myōe (1173–1232). When I am asked for specimens of my handwriting, it is these poems that I often choose.

The second poem bears an unusually detailed account of its origins, such as to be an explanation of the heart of its meaning: "On the night of the twelfth day of the twelfth month of the year 1224,* the moon was behind clouds. I sat in Zen meditation in the Kakyū

---

* By lunar reckoning.

Hall. When the hour of the midnight vigil came, I ceased meditation and descended from the hall on the peak to the lower quarters, and as I did so the moon came from the clouds and set the snow to glowing. The moon was my companion, and not even the wolf howling in the valley brought fear. When, presently, I came out of the lower quarters again, the moon was again behind clouds. As the bell was signaling the late-night vigil, I climbed once more to the peak, and the moon saw me on the way. I entered the meditation hall, and the moon, chasing the clouds, was about to sink behind the far peak, and it seemed to me that it was keeping me secret company."

There follows the poem I have quoted, and, with the explanation that it was composed as Myōe entered the meditation hall after watching the moon sink toward the mountain, there comes yet another poem:

> *"I shall go behind the mountain.*
> *Go there too, O moon.*
> *Night after night we shall keep each*
> *other company."*

Here is the setting for another poem, after Myōe had spent the rest of the night in the meditation hall, or perhaps gone there again before dawn: "Opening my eyes from my meditations, I saw the moon in the dawn, lighting the window. In a dark place myself, I felt as if my own heart were glowing with light which seemed to be that of the moon:

> *"My heart shines, a pure expanse*
> *of light;*
> *And no doubt the moon will think*
> *the light its own."*

Because of such a spontaneous and innocent stringing together of mere ejaculations as the following, Myōe has been called the poet of the moon:

"*O bright, bright,*
O bright, bright, bright,
O bright, bright.
Bright, O bright, bright,
Bright, O bright moon."

In his three poems on the winter moon, from late night into the dawn, Myōe follows entirely the bent of Saigyō, another poet-priest, who lived from 1118 to 1190: "Though I compose poetry, I do not think of it as composed poetry." The thirty-one syllables of each poem, honest and straightforward as if he were addressing the moon, are not merely to "the moon as my companion." Seeing the moon, he becomes the moon, the moon seen by him becomes him. He sinks into nature, becomes one with nature. The light of the "clear heart" of the priest, seated in the meditation hall in the darkness before the dawn, becomes for the dawn moon its own light.

As we see from the long introduction to the first of Myōe's poems quoted above, in which the winter moon becomes a companion, the heart of the priest, sunk in meditation upon religion and philosophy, there in the mountain hall, is engaged in a delicate interplay and exchange with the moon; and it is this of which the poet sings. My reason for choosing that first poem when asked for a specimen of my handwriting has to do with its remarkable gentleness and compassion. Winter moon, going behind the clouds and coming forth again, making bright my footsteps as I go to the meditation hall and descend again, making me unafraid of the wolf: does not the wind sink into you, does not the snow, are you not cold? I choose it as a poem of warm, deep, delicate compassion, a poem that has in it the deep quiet of the Japanese spirit. Dr. Yashiro Yukio, internationally known as a scholar of Botticelli, a man of great learning in the art of the past and the present, of the East and the West, has said that one of the special characteristics of Japanese art can be summed up in a single poetic sentence: "The time of the snows, of the moon, of the blossoms —then more than ever we think of our comrades." When we see the beauty of the snow, when we see the beauty of the full moon, when we see the beauty of the cherries in bloom, when in short we brush against and are awakened by the beauty of the four seasons, it is then that we think most of those close to us, and want them to share the pleasure. The excitement of beauty calls forth strong fellow feelings, yearnings for companionship, and the word "comrade" can be taken to mean "human being." The snow, the moon, the blossoms, words expressive of the seasons as they move one into another, include in the Japanese tradition the beauty of mountains and rivers and grasses and trees, of all the myriad manifestations of nature, of human feelings as well. That spirit, that feeling for one's comrades in the snow, the moonlight, under the blossoms, is also basic to the tea ceremony. A tea ceremony is a coming together in feeling, a meeting of good comrades in a good season. I may say in passing that to see my novel *Thousand Cranes* as an evocation of the formal and spiritual beauty of the tea ceremony is a misreading. It is a negative work, an expression of doubt about and a warning against the vulgarity into which the tea ceremony has fallen.

> "*In the spring, cherry blossoms,*
> *in the summer the cuckoo.*
> *In autumn the moon, and in winter*
> *the snow, clear, cold.*"

One can, if one chooses, see in Dōgen's poem about the beauty of the four seasons no more than a conventional, ordinary, mediocre stringing together, in a most awkward form, of representative images from the four seasons.   One can see it as a poem that is not really a poem at all.   And yet very similar is the deathbed poem of the priest Ryōkan (1758–1831):

> "*What shall be my legacy?*
> *The blossoms of spring,*
> *The cuckoo in the hills,*
> *the leaves of autumn.*"

In this poem, as in Dōgen's, the commonest of figures and the commonest of words are strung together without hesitation—no, to particular effect, rather—and so they transmit the very essence of Japan. And it is Ryōkan's last poem that I have quoted.

> "*A long, misty day in spring:*
> *I saw it to a close, playing ball*
> *with the children.*"

> "*The breeze is fresh,*
> *the moon is clear.*
> *Together let us dance the night*
> *away, in what is left of old age.*"

> "*It is not that I wish to have none*
> *of the world,*
> *It is that I am better at the*
> *pleasure enjoyed alone.*"

Ryōkan, who shook off the modern **vulgarity** of his day, who was immersed in the elegance of earlier centuries, and whose poetry and calligraphy are much admired in Japan today—he lived in the spirit of these poems, a wanderer down country paths, a grass hut for shelter, rags for clothes, farmers to talk to. The profundity of religion and literature was not, for him, in the abstruse. He rather pursued literature and belief in the benign spirit summarized in the Buddhist phrase "a smiling face and gentle words." In his last poem he offered nothing as a legacy. He but hoped that after his death nature would remain beautiful. That could be his bequest. One feels in the poem the emotions of old Japan, and the heart of a religious faith as well.

> *"I wondered and wondered when*
> *she would come.*
> *And now we are together.*
> *What thoughts need I have?"*

Ryōkan wrote love poetry too. This is an example of which I am fond. An old man of sixty-nine* (I might point out that at the same age I am the recipient of the Nobel Prize), Ryōkan met a twenty-nine-year old nun named Teishin, and was blessed with love. The poem can be seen as one of happiness at having met the ageless woman, of happiness at having met the one for whom the wait was so long. The last line is simplicity itself.

Ryōkan died at the age of seventy-four. He was born in the province of Echigo, the present Niigata Prefecture and the setting for my novel *Snow Country*, a northerly region on what is known as the reverse side of Japan, where cold winds come down across the Japan Sea from Siberia. He lived his whole life in the snow country, and to his "eyes in their last extremity," when he was old

---

* By the Oriental way of counting. Sixty-seven or sixty-eight by the Western. A year or two should also be subtracted from Teishin's age, and the count at Ryōkan's death.

and tired and knew that death was near, and had attained enlightenment, the snow country, as we see in his last poem, was yet more beautiful, I should imagine. I have an essay with the title "Eyes in their Last Extremity." The title comes from the suicide note of the short-story writer Akutagawa Ryūnosuke (1892–1927). It is the phrase that pulls at me with the greatest strength. Akutagawa said that he seemed to be gradually losing the animal something known as the power to live, and continued:

"I am living in a world of morbid nerves, clear and cold as ice.... I do not know when I will summon up the resolve to kill myself. But nature is for me more beautiful than it has ever been before. I have no doubt that you will laugh at the contradiction, for here I love nature even when I am contemplating suicide. But nature is beautiful because it comes to my eyes in their last extremity."

Akutagawa committed suicide in 1927, at the age of thirty-five.

In my essay "Eyes in their Last Extremity," I had this to say: "However alienated one may be from the world, suicide is not a form of enlightenment. However admirable he may be, the man who commits suicide is far from the realm of the saint." I neither admire nor am in sympathy with suicide. I had another friend who died young, an avant-garde painter. He too thought of suicide over the years, and of him I wrote in this same essay: "He seems to have said over and over that there is no art superior to death, that to die is to live." I could see, however, that for him, born in a Buddhist temple and educated in a Buddhist school, the concept of death was very different from that in the West. "Among those who give thoughts to things, is there one who does not think of suicide?" With me was the knowledge that that fellow Ikkyū (1394–1481) twice contemplated suicide. I have said "that fellow," because the priest Ikkyū is known even to children as a most witty and amusing person, and because anecdotes about his limitlessly eccentric behavior have come down to us in ample numbers. It is said of him that children climbed his knee to stroke his beard, that wild birds took feed from his hand. It would seem from all this that he was the ultimate in mindlessness, that he was an approachable and gentle sort of priest. As a matter of fact he was the most severe and profound of Zen priests. Said to have been the son of an emperor, he entered a temple at the age of six,* and

* Again, by Oriental count.

early showed genius as a poetic prodigy. At the same time he was troubled with the deepest of doubts about religion and life. "If there is a god, let him help me. If there is none, let me throw myself to the bottom of the lake and become food for fishes." Leaving behind these words he sought to throw himself into a lake, but was held back. On another occasion, numbers of his fellows were incriminated when a priest in his Daitokuji Temple committed suicide. Ikkyū went back to the temple, "the burden heavy on my shoulders," and sought to starve himself to death. He gave his collected poetry the title "Collection of the Roiling Clouds," and himself used the expression "Roiling Clouds" as a pen name. In this collection and its successor are poems quite without parallel in the Chinese and especially the Zen poetry of the Japanese middle ages, erotic poems and poems about the secrets of the bedchamber that leave one in utter astonishment. He sought, by eating fish and drinking spirits and having commerce with women, to go beyond the rules and proscriptions of the Zen of his day, to seek liberation from them; and thus, turning against established religious forms, he sought in the pursuit of Zen the revival and affirmation of the essence of life, of human existence, in a day of civil war and moral collapse.

His temple, the Daitokuji at Murasakino in Kyoto, remains a center of the tea ceremony, and specimens of his calligraphy are greatly admired as hangings in alcoves of tea rooms. I myself have two specimens of Ikkyū's calligraphy. One of them is a single line: "It is easy to enter the world of the Buddha, it is hard to enter the world of the devil." Much drawn to these words, I frequently make use of them when asked for a specimen of my own writing. They can be read in any number of ways, as difficult as one chooses, but in that world of the devil added to the world of the Buddha, Ikkyū of Zen comes home to me with great immediacy. The fact that for an artist, seeking truth, good, and beauty, the fear and petition even as a prayer in those words about the world of the devil —the fact that it should be there apparent on the surface, hidden behind, perhaps speaks with the inevitability of fate. And the devil's world is the world difficult of entry. It is not for the weak of heart.

> *"If you meet a Buddha, kill him. If you meet a patriarch of the law, kill him."*

This is a well-known Zen motto. If Buddhism is divided generally into the sects that believe in salvation by faith and those that believe in salvation by one's own efforts, then of course there must be such violent utterances in Zen, which insists upon salvation by one's own efforts. On the other side, the side of salvation by faith, Shinran (1173–1262), the founder of the Shin sect, once said: "The good shall be reborn in paradise, and how much more shall that be the case with the bad." This view of things has something in common with Ikkyū's world of the Buddha and world of the devil, and yet at heart the two have their different inclinations. Shinran also said: "I shall take not a single disciple."

"If you meet a Buddha, kill him. If you meet a patriarch of the law, kill him." "I shall not take a single disciple." In these two statements, perhaps, is the rigorous fate of art.

In Zen there is no worship of images. Zen does have images, but in the hall where the regimen of meditation is pursued, there are neither images nor pictures of Buddhas, nor are there scriptures. The Zen disciple sits for long hours silent and motionless, with his eyes closed. Presently he enters a state of impassivity, free from all ideas and all thoughts. He departs from the self and enters the realm of nothingness. This is not the nothingness or the emptiness of the West. It is rather the reverse, a universe of the spirit in which everything communicates freely with everything, transcending bounds, limitless. There are of course masters of Zen, and the disciple is brought toward enlightenment by exchanging questions and answers with his master, and he studies the scriptures. The disciple must, however, always be lord of his own thoughts, and must attain enlightenment through his own efforts. And the emphasis is less upon reason and argument than upon intuition, immediate feeling. Enlightenment comes not from teaching but through the eye awakened inwardly. Truth is in "the discarding of words," it lies "outside words." And so we have the extreme of "silence like thunder," in the Vimalakīrti Mirdeśa Sūtra. Tradition has it that Bodhidharma, a southern Indian prince who lived in about the sixth century and was the founder of Zen in China, sat for nine years in silence facing the wall of a cave, and finally attained enlightenment. The Zen practice of sitting in silent meditation derives from Bodhidharma.

Here are two religious poems by Ikkyū:

"*When I ask you answer.*
When I do not you do not.

What is there then in your heart,
O Lord Bodhidharma?"

"And what is it, the heart?
It is the sound of the pine breeze
there in the painting."

Here we have the spirit of Oriental painting. The heart of ink painting is in space, abbreviation, what is left undrawn. In the words of the Chinese painter Chin Nung: "You paint the branch well, and you hear the sound of the wind." And the priest Dōgen once more: "Are there not these cases? Enlightenment in the voice of the bamboo. Radiance of heart in the peach blossom."

Ikenobō Sen'ō, a master of flower arranging, once said (the remark is to be found in his "secret pronouncements"): "With a spray of flowers, a bit of water, one evokes the vastness of rivers and mountains. To the instant are brought all the manifold delights. Verily, it is like the sorcery of the wizard." The Japanese garden too, of course, symbolizes the vastness of nature. The Western garden tends to be symmetrical, the Japanese garden asymmetrical, for the asymmetrical has the greater power to symbolize multiplicity and vastness. The asymmetry, of course, rests upon a balance imposed by delicate sensibilities. Nothing is more complicated, varied, attentive to detail than the Japanese art of landscape gardening. Thus there is the form called the dry landscape, composed entirely of rocks, in which the arrangement of the rocks gives expression to mountains and rivers that are not present, and even suggests the waves of the great ocean breaking in upon cliffs. Compressed to the ultimate, the Japanese garden becomes the *bonsai* dwarf garden, or the *bonseki*, its dry version.

In the Oriental word for landscape, literally "mountain-water," with its related implications in landscape painting and landscape gardening, there is contained the concept of the sere and wasted, and even of the sad and the threadbare. Yet in the sad, austere, autumnal qualities so valued by the tea ceremony, itself summarized in the expression "gently respectful, cleanly quiet," there lies concealed a great richness of spirit; and the tea room, so rigidly confined and simple, contains boundless space and unlimited elegance. The single flower contains more brightness than a hundred flowers. The great sixteenth-century master of the tea ceremony and flower arranging, Rikyū, taught that it was wrong to use fully opened flowers. Even in the tea ceremony today the general practice is to have in the alcove of the tea room but a single flower, and that a flower in bud. In winter a special flower of winter, let us say a camellia, bearing some such name as White Jewel or Wabisuke, which might be translated literally as "Helpmate in Solitude," is chosen, a camellia remarkable among camellias for its whiteness and the smallness of its blossoms; and but a single bud is set out in the alcove. White is the cleanest of colors, it contains in itself all the other colors. And there must always be dew on the bud. The bud is moistened with a few drops of water. The most splendid of arrangements for the tea ceremony comes in May, when a peony is put out in a celadon vase; but here again there is a single bud, always with dew upon it. Not only are there drops of water upon the flower, the vase too is frequently moistened.

Among flower vases, the ware that is given the highest rank is old Iga, from the fifteenth and sixteenth centuries, and it commands the highest price. When old Iga has been dampened, its colors and its glow take on a beauty such as to awaken one afresh. Iga was fired at very high temperatures. The straw ash and the smoke from the fuel fell and flowed against the surface, and, as the temperature dropped, became a sort of glaze. Because the colors were not fabricated but were rather the result of nature at work in the kiln, color patterns emerged in such varieties as to be called quirks and freaks of the kiln. The rough, austere, strong surfaces of old Iga take on a voluptuous glow when dampened. It breathes to the rhythm of the dew of the flowers.

The taste of the tea ceremony also asks that the tea bowl be moistened before using, to bring forth its own soft glow.

Ikenobō Sen'ō remarked on another occasion (this too is in his "secret pronouncements") that "the mountains and strands should appear in their own forms." Bringing a new spirit into his school of flower arranging, therefore, he found "flowers" in broken vessels and withered branches, and in them too the enlightenment that comes from flowers. "The ancients arranged flowers and pursued enlightenment." Here we see an awakening to the heart of the Japanese spirit, under the influence of Zen. And here too, perhaps, is the heart of a man living in the devastation of long civil wars.

The Tales of Ise, compiled in the tenth century, is the oldest Japanese collection of lyrical episodes, numbers of which might be called short stories. In one of them we learn that the poet Ariwara no

Yukihira, having invited guests, put in flowers:

"Being a man of feeling, he had in a large jar a most unusual wistaria. The trailing spray of flowers was upwards of three and a half feet long."

A spray of wistaria of such length is indeed so unusual as to make one have doubts about the credibility of the writer; and yet I can feel in this great spray a symbol of Heian culture. The wistaria is a very Japanese flower, and it has a feminine elegance. Wistaria sprays, as they trail in the breeze, suggest softness, gentleness, reticence. Disappearing and then appearing again in the early summer greenery, they have in them that feeling for the poignant beauty of things long characterized by the Japanese as *mono no aware*. No doubt there was a particular splendor in that spray upwards of three and a half feet long. The splendors of Heian culture a millennium ago and the emergence of a peculiarly Japanese beauty were as wondrous as this "most unusual wistaria", for the culture of T'ang China had at length been absorbed and Japanized. In poetry there came, early in the tenth century, the first of the imperially commissioned anthologies, the *Kokinshū*, and in fiction the *Tales of Ise*, followed by the supreme masterpieces of classical Japanese prose, the *Tale of Genji* of Lady Murasaki and the *Pillow Book* of Sei Shōnagon, both of whom lived from the late tenth century into the early eleventh. So was established a tradition which influenced and even controlled Japanese literature for eight hundred years. The *Tale of Genji* in particular is the highest pinnacle of Japanese literature. Even down to our day there has not been a piece of fiction to compare with it. That such a modern work should have been written in the eleventh century is a miracle, and as a miracle the work is widely known abroad. Although my grasp of classical Japanese was uncertain, the Heian classics were my principal boyhood reading, and it is the *Genji*, I think, that has meant the most to me. For centuries after it was written, fascination with the *Genji* persisted, and imitations and reworkings did homage to it. The *Genji* was a wide and deep source of nourishment for poetry, of course, and for the fine arts and handicrafts as well, and even for landscape gardening.

Murasaki and Sei Shōnagon, and such famous poets as Izumi Shikibu, who probably died early in the eleventh century, and Akazome Emon, who probably died in the mid eleventh century, were all ladies-in-waiting in the imperial court. Japanese culture was court culture, and court culture was feminine. The day of the *Genji* and the *Pillow Book* was its finest, when ripeness was moving into decay. One feels the sadness at the end of glory, the high tide of Japanese court culture. The court went into its decline, power moved from the court nobility to the military aristocracy, in whose hands it remained through almost seven centuries from the founding of the Kamakura Shogunate in 1192 to the Meiji Restoration in 1867 and 1868. It is not to be thought, however, that either the imperial institution or court culture vanished. In the eighth of the imperial anthologies, the *Shinkokinshū* of the early thirteenth century, the technical dexterity of the *Kokinshū* was pushed yet a step further, and sometimes fell into mere verbal dalliance; but there were added elements of the mysterious, the suggestive, the evocative and inferential, elements of sensuous fantasy that have something in common with modern symbolist poetry. Saigyō, who has been mentioned earlier, was a representative poet linking the two ages, Heian and Kamakura.

> *"Did I dream of him because I*
> *longed for him?*
> *Had I known it to be a dream,*
> *I should not have wished to*
> *awaken."*

> *"In my dreams I go to him each*
> *night without fail.*
> *But my dreams are less than a*
> *single glimpse in the waking."*

These are by Ono no Komachi, the leading poetess of the *Kokinshū*, who sings of dreams, even, with a straightforward realism. But when we come to the

following poems of the Empress Eifuku
(1271–1342), from the late Kamakura
and early Muromachi periods, some-
what later than the *Shinkokinshū*, we have
a more subtle realism.   It becomes a
symbol of a delicately Japanese mel-
ancholy, and seems to me more modern:

> *"Shining upon the bamboo thicket*
> *where the sparrows twitter,*
> *The sunlight takes on the color of*
> *the autumn."*

> *"The hagi* falls, the autumn*
> *wind is piercing.*
> *Upon the wall, the evening sun*
> *disappears."*

Dōgen, whose poem about the clear,
cold snow I have quoted, and Myōe,
who wrote of the winter moon as his
companion, were of generally the *Shinkokinshū* period.   Myōe exchanged poems

---

* Lespedeza japonica.

with Saigyō and the two discussed poetry together. The following is from the biography of Myōe by his disciple Kikai:

"Saigyō frequently came and talked of poetry. His own view of poetry, he said, was far from the ordinary. Cherry blossoms, the cuckoo, the moon, snow: confronted with all the varied forms of nature, his eyes and his ears were filled with emptiness. And were not the words that came forth true words? When he sang of the blossoms, the blossoms were not on his mind, when he sang of the moon he did not think of the moon. As the occasion presented itself, as the urge arose, he wrote poetry. The red rainbow across the sky was as the sky taking on color. The white sunlight was as the sky growing bright. Yet the empty sky, by its nature, was not something to become bright. It was not

something to take on color. With a
spirit like the empty sky he gave color to
all the varied scenes, but not a trace
remained. In such poetry was the
Buddha, the manifestation of the ultimate truth."

Here we have the emptiness, the
nothingness, of the Orient. My own
works have been described as works of
emptiness, but it is not to be taken for
the nihilism of the West. The spiritual
foundation would seem to be quite
different. Dōgen entitled his poem
about the seasons "Innate Reality," and
even as he sang of the beauty of the
seasons he was deeply immersed in Zen.

永福門院

鎌倉時代末期の女流歌人。伏見天皇の中宮。歌風は、『万葉集』の素朴性と『新古今集』の艶な要素を含み典雅である。自然を詠んだ作品に秀歌が多いが、叙情歌にも情熱的な作がある。

美しい日本の私
その序説

川端康成著
サイデンステッカー訳

著者川端康成は、一八九九年、大阪に生まれた。一九二四年に、東京帝国大学国文科卒。小説『伊豆の踊子』『雪国』等を経て戦後は、『千羽鶴』『山の音』『古都』『眠れる美女』を発表。一九四八年から一九六五年まで、日本ペンクラブ会長。一九五三年から芸術院会員。一九六一年に文化勲章受章。一九六八年にノーベル文学賞受賞。

訳者エドワード・G・サイデンステッカーは、一九二一年、アメリカ合衆国コロラドに生まれた。コロラド大学卒業後、コロンビア大学・ハーバード大学・東京大学の各大学院で日本文学を専攻。現在、ミシガン大学教授。専門は日本文学の翻訳と批評。翻訳に川端康成著『雪国』『千羽鶴』、谷崎潤一郎著『細雪』『蓼喰ふ虫』、古典の『蜻蛉日記』などがあり、評論に『永井荷風論』がある。

美しい日本の私

川端康成

春は花夏ほととぎす秋は月

冬雪さえて冷しかりけり

と、

道元禅師*（一二〇〇年—五三年）の「本来ノ面目」と題するこの歌

雲を出でて我にともなふ冬の月

風や身にしむ雪や冷めたき

明恵上人*（一一七三年—一二三二年）のこの歌とを、私は揮毫をも

とめられた折りに書くことがあります。

明恵のこの歌には、歌物語と言へるほどの、長く詳しい詞書きが

あって、歌のこころを明らかにしてゐます。

元仁元年（一二二四年）十二月十二日の夜、天くもり月くらき
に花宮殿に入りて座禅す。やうやく中夜にいたりて、出観の
後、峰の房より下房へ帰る時、月雲間より出でて、光り雪にか
がやく。狼の谷に吼ゆるも、月を友として、いと恐ろしから
ず。下房に入りて後、また立ち出でたれば、月また曇りにけ
り。かくしつつ後夜の鐘の音聞こゆれば、また峰の房へのぼる
に、月もまた雲より出でて道を送る。峰にいたりて禅堂に入ら
んとする時、月また雲を追ひ来て、向ふの峰にかくれんとする
よそほひ、人しれず月の我にともなふかと見ゆれば、

この歌。それにつづけて、

山の端に傾ぶくを見おきて峰の禅堂にいたる時、

山の端にわれも入りなむ月も入れ
夜な夜なごとにまた友とせむ

堂に入ったかして、

明恵は禅堂に夜通しこもってゐたか、あるひは夜明け前にまた禅

禅観のひまに眼を開けば、有明けの月の光、窓の前にさしたり。我身は
暗きところにて見やりたれば、澄める心、月の光に紛るる心地すれば、

隈もなく澄める心の輝けば
我が光とや月思ふらむ

西行を桜の詩人といふことがあるのに対して、明恵を「月の歌

人」と呼ぶ人もあるほどで、

あかあかやあかあかあかやあかあかや

あかやあかあかあかあかあかや月

と、ただ感動の声をそのまま連ねた歌があったりしますが、夜半か
ら暁までの「冬の月」の三首にしても、「歌を詠むとも実に歌と
も思はず」（西行の言）の趣きで、素直、純真、月に話しかける言
葉そのままの三十一文字で、いはゆる「月を友とする」よりも月に
親しく、月を見る我が月になり、我に見られる月が我になり、自然
に没入、自然と合一してゐます。暁前の暗い禅堂に座って思索する
僧の「澄める心」の光りを、有明けの月は月自身の光りと思ふだら
うといふ風であります。

「我にともなふ冬の月」の歌も、長い詞書きに明らかのやうに、明恵が山の禅堂に入って、宗教、哲学の思索をする心と、月が微妙に相応じ相交はるのを歌ってゐるのですが、私がこれを借りて揮毫しますのは、まことに心やさしい、思ひやりの歌とも受け取れるからであります。雲に入ったり雲を出たりして、禅堂に行き帰りする我の足もとを明るくしてくれ、狼の吼え声もこはいと感じさせないでくれる「冬の月」よ、風が身にしみないか、雪が冷めたくないか。私はこれを自然、そして人間にたいする、あたたかく、深い、こまやかな思ひやりの歌として、しみじみとやさしい日本人の心の歌として、人に書いてあげてゐます。

そのボッティチェリの研究が世界に知られ、古今東西の美術に博

識の矢代幸雄博士も「日本美術の特質」の一つを「雪月花の時、最も友を思ふ。」という詩語に約められるとしてゐます。雪の美しいのを見るにつけ、月の美しいのを見るにつけ、つまり四季折り折りの美に、自分が触れ目覚める時、美にめぐりあふ幸ひを得た時には、親しい友が切に思はれ、このよろこびを共にしたいと願ふ、つまり、美の感動が人なつかしい思ひやりを強く誘ひ出すのです。この「友」は、広く「人間」ともとれませう。また「雪、月、花」といふ四季の移りの折り折りの美を現はす言葉は、日本においては山川草木、森羅万象、自然のすべて、そして人間感情をも含めての、美を現はす言葉とするのが伝統なのであります。そして日本の茶道も、「雪月花の時、最も友をおもふ」のがその根本の心で、茶会はその「感会」、

よい時によい友どちが集ふよい会なのであります。——ちなみに、私の小説『千羽鶴』は、日本の茶の心と形の美しさを書いたと読まれるのは誤りで、今の世間に俗悪となった茶、それに疑ひと警めを向けた、むしろ否定の作品なのです。

　　春は花夏ほととぎす秋は月
　　冬雪さえて冷しかりけり

この道元の歌も四季の美の歌で、古来の日本人が春、夏、秋、冬に、第一に愛でる自然の景物の代表を、ただ四つ無造作にならべただけの、月並み、常套、平凡、この上ないと思へば思へ、歌になってゐない歌と言へば言へます。しかし別の古人の似た歌の一つ、僧

良寛（一七五八年―一八三一年）の辞世、

　形見とて何か残さん春は花

　山ほととぎす秋はもみぢ葉

　これも道元の歌と同じやうに、ありきたりの事柄とありふれた言葉を、ためらひもなく、と言ふよりも、ことさらもとめて、連ねて重ねるうちに、日本の真髄を伝へたのであります。まして、良寛の歌は辞世です。

　　霞立つ永き春日を子供らと

　　手毬つきつつこの日暮らしつ

風は清し月はさやけしいざ共に

踊り明かさむ老いの名残りに

世の中にまじらぬとにはあらねども

ひとり遊びぞ我はまされる

これらの歌のやうな心と暮らし、草の庵に住み、粗衣をまとひ、野道をさまよひ歩いては、子供と遊び、農夫と語り、信教と文学との深さを、むづかしい話にはしないで、「和顔愛語」の無垢な言行とし、しかも、詩歌と書風と共に、江戸後期、十八世紀の終りから十九世紀の始め、日本の近世の俗習を超脱、古代の高雅に通達して、現代の日本でもその書と詩歌をはなはだ貴ばれてゐる良寛、その人

14

の辞世が、自分は形見に残すものはなにも持たぬし、なにも残せるとは思はぬが、自分の死後も自然はなほ美しい、これがただ自分のこの世に残す形見になってくれるだらう、といふ歌であったのです。日本古来の心情がこもってゐるとともに、良寛の宗教の心も聞える歌です。

いついつと待ちにし人は来りけり
今は相見てなにか思はん

このやうな愛の歌も良寛にはあって、私の好きな歌ですが、老衰の加はった六十八歳の良寛は、二十九歳の若い尼、貞心とめぐりあって、うるはしい愛にめぐまれます。永遠の女性にめぐりあへたよろ

こびの歌とも、待ちわびた愛人が来てくれたよろこびの歌とも取れます。「今は相見てなにか思はん」が素直に満ちてゐます。

良寛は七十四歳で死にました。私の小説の『雪国』と同じ雪国の越後、つまり、シベリアから日本海を渡って来る寒風に真向ひの、裏日本の北国、今の新潟県に生まれて、生涯をその雪国に過ごしたのでしたが、老い衰へて、死の近いのを知った、そして心がさとりに澄み渡ってゐた、この詩僧の「末期の眼＊」には、辞世にある、雪国の自然がなほ美しく映ったであらうと思ひます。私に『末期の眼』といふ随筆がありますが、ここでの「末期の眼」といふ言葉は、芥川龍之介（一八九二年―一九二七年）の自殺の遺書から拾ったものでした。その遺書のなかで、殊に私の心を惹いた言葉です。

「所謂生活力といふ」、「動物力」を「次第に失ってゐるであらう」、僕の今住んでゐるのは氷のやうに透み渡った、病的な神経の世界である。〈中略〉僕がいつ敢然と自殺出来るかは疑問である。唯自然はかういふ僕にはいつもよりも一層美しい。君は自然の美しいのを愛ししかも自殺しようとする僕の矛盾を笑ふであらう。けれども自然の美しいのは、僕の末期の眼に映るからである。

一九二七年、芥川は三十五歳で自殺しました。私は『末期の眼』のなかにも「いかに現世を厭離するとも、自殺はさとりの姿ではない。いかに徳行高くとも、自殺者は大聖の域に遠い」と書いてゐまして、芥川やまた戦後の太宰治（一九〇九年—四八年）などの自殺を

讃美するものでも、共感するものでもありません。しかし、これも若く死んだ友人、日本での前衛画家の一人は、やはり年久しく自殺を思ひ「死にまさる芸術はないとか、死ぬることは生きることだとかは、口癖のやうだったさう」（『末期の眼』）ですが、仏教の寺院に生まれ、仏教の学校を出たこの人の死の見方は、西洋の死の考へ方とはちがってゐただらうと、私は推察したものでした。「もの思ふ人、誰か自殺を思はざる。」でせうが、そのことで私の胸にある一つは、あの一休禅師（一三九四年―一四八一年）が、二度も自殺を企てたと知ったことであります。

　ここで一休を「あの」と言ひましたのは、童話の頓智和尚として子供たちにも知られ、無礙奔放な奇行の逸話が広く伝はってゐるか

らです。「童児が膝にのぼって、ひげを撫で、野鳥も一休の手から餌を啄む。」といふ風で、これは無心の極みのさま、そして親しみやすくやさしい僧のやうですが、実はまことに峻厳深念な禅の僧であったのです。天皇の御子であるとも言はれる一休は、六歳で寺に入り、天才少年詩人のひらめきも見せながら、宗教と人生の根本の疑惑に悩み「神あらば我を救へ。神なくんば我を湖底に沈めて、魚の腹を肥せ。」と、湖に身を投げようとして引きとめられたことがあります。また後に、一休の大徳寺の一人の僧が自殺したために、数人の僧が獄につながれた時、一休は責任を感じて「肩の上重く」、山に入って、食を絶ち、死を決したこともあります。

一休はその「詩集」を自分で『狂雲集』と名づけ、狂雲とも号し

ました。そして『狂雲集』とその続集には、日本の中世の漢詩、殊に禅僧の詩としては、類ひを絶し、おどろきに胆をつぶすほどの恋愛詩、閨房の秘事までをあらはにした艶詩が見えます。一休は魚を食ひ、酒を飲み、女色を近づけ、禅の戒律、禁制を超越し、それらから自分を解放することによって、そのころの宗教の形骸に反逆し、そのころ戦乱で崩壊の世道人心のなかに、人間の実存、生命の本然の復活、確立を志したのでせう。

一休のゐた京都紫野の大徳寺は、今日も茶道の本山のさまです し、一休の墨蹟も茶室の掛け物として貴ばれてゐます。私も一休の書を二幅所蔵してゐます。その一幅は、「仏界入り易く、魔界入り難し。」と一行書きです。私はこの言葉に惹かれますから、自分で

20

もよくこの言葉を揮毫します。意味はいろいろに読まれ、またむづ
かしく考へれば限りがないでせうが「仏界入り易し」につづけて
「魔界入り難し」と言ひ加へた、その禅の一休が私の胸に来ます。
究極は真・善・美を目ざす芸術家にも「魔界入り難し」の願ひ、恐
れの、祈りに通ふ思ひが、表にあらはれ、あるひは裏にひそむの
は、運命の必然でありませう。「魔界」なくして「仏界」はありま
せん。そして「魔界」に入る方がむづかしいのです。心弱くてでき
ることではありません。

　　逢レ仏殺レ仏ヲ　　逢レ祖殺レ祖ヲ

これはよく知られた禅語ですが、他力本願と自力本願とに仏教の

宗派を分けると、勿論自力の禅宗にはこのやうに激しくきびしい言葉もあるわけです。他力本願の真宗の親鸞（一一七三年―一二六二年）の「善人往生す。いはんや悪人をや。」も、一休の「仏界」「魔界」と通ふ心もありますが、行きちがふ心もあります。その親鸞も「弟子一人持たず候」と言ってゐます。「祖に逢へば祖を殺し」、「弟子一人持たず」は、また芸術の厳烈な運命でありませう。

禅宗に偶像崇拝はありません。禅寺にも仏像はありますけれども、修行の場、坐禅して思索する堂には仏像、仏画はなく、経文の備へもなく、瞑目して、長い時間、無言、不動で座ってゐるのです。そして、無念無想の境に入るのです。「我」をなくして「無」になるのです。この「無」は西洋風の虚無ではなく、むしろその逆

で、万有が自在に通ふ空、無涯無辺、無尽蔵の心の宇宙なのです。

禅でも師に指導され、師と問答して啓発され、禅の古典を習学するのは勿論ですが、思索の主はあくまで自己、さとりは自分ひとりの力でひらかねばならないのです。そして、論理よりも直観です。他からの教へよりも、内に目ざめるさとりです。真理は、「不立文字（ふりふもんじ）」であり「言外（げんぐわい）」にあります。維摩居士（ゆるまこじ）の「黙如レ雷（もくジョライ）」まで極まりもしませう。中国の禅宗の始祖、達磨大師（だるま）は「面壁九年（めんぺきくねん）」と言ひまして、洞窟の岩壁に向って九年間座りつづけながら、沈思黙考の果に、さとりに達したと伝へられてゐます。禅の坐禅はこの達磨の坐禅から来てゐます。

問へば言ふ問はねば言はぬ達磨どの
　心の内になにかあるべき　　（一休）

また、同じ一休の道歌

心とはいかなるものを言ふならん
　墨絵に書きし松風の音

これは東洋画の精神でもあります。東洋画の空間、余白、省筆も、
この墨絵の心でありませう。「能畫ニ一枝ヲ風有リレ聲」（金冬心＊）です。
道元禅師にも「見ずや、竹の声に道を悟り、桃の花に心を明るむ。」
との言葉があります。日本の花道、生け花の名家の池坊専応（一五

24

三三年―一五五四年）も、その「口伝」に「ただ小水尺樹をもって、江山数程の勝機（おもむき）を現はし、暫時傾刻のあひだに、千変万化の佳興をもよほす。あたかも仙家の妙術と言ひつべし」と言ってゐます。日本の庭園もまた大きい自然を象徴するものです。西洋の庭園が多くは均整に造られるのにくらべて、日本の庭園はたいてい不均整に造られますが、不均整は均整よりも、多くのもの、広いものを象徴出来るからでありませう。勿論その不均整は、日本人の繊細微妙な感性によって釣り合ひが保たれての上であります。日本の造園ほど複雑、多趣、綿密、したがってむづかしい造園法はありません。「枯山水」といふ、岩や石を組み合はせるだけの法は、その「石組み」によって、そこにない山や川、また大海の波の打ち寄

せるさままでを現はします。その凝縮を極めると、日本の盆栽となり、盆石となります。「山水」といふ言葉には、山と水、つまり自然の景色、山水画、つまり風景画、庭園などの意味から、「ものさびたさま」とか、「さびしく、みすぼらしいこと」とかの意味まであります。しかし「和敬清寂」の茶道が尊ぶ「わび・さび」は、勿論むしろ心の豊かさを蔵してのことですし、極めて狭小、簡素の茶室は、かへって無辺の広さと無限の優麗とを宿してをります。

一輪の花は百輪の花よりも花やかさを思はせるのです。開き切った花を活けてはならぬと、利休も教へてゐますが、今日の日本の茶でも、茶室の床にはただ一輪の花、しかもつぼみを生けることが多いのであります。冬ですと、冬の季節の花、たとへば「白玉」とか

「侘助」とか名づけられた椿、椿の種類のうちでも花の小さい椿、その白をえらび、ただ一つのつぼみを生けます。色のない白は最も清らかであるとともに、最も多くの色を持ってゐます。そして、そのつぼみには必ず露をふくませます。幾滴かの水で花を濡らしておくのです。五月、牡丹の花を青磁の花瓶に生けるのは茶の花として最も豪華ですが、その牡丹はやはり白のつぼみ一つ、そしてやはり露をふくませます。花に水のしづくを添へるばかりではなく、花生けもあらかじめ水に濡らしておく焼きものが少くありません。

日本の焼きものの花生けのなかで、最も位が高いとし、また価ひも高い、古伊賀（およそ十五、六世紀）は水に濡らして、はじめて目ざめるやうに、美しい生色を放ちます。伊賀は強い火度で焼きます

が、その焚きもの（燃料）の藁灰や煙が降りかかって花瓶の体に着いたり流れたりで、火度のさがるにしたがって、それが釉薬のやうになるのです。陶工による人工ではなく、窯のなかの自然のわざですから、窯変と言ってもいいやうな、さまざまな色模様が生まれます。その伊賀焼きの渋くて、粗くて、強い肌が、水気を含むと、艶な照りを見せます。花の露とも呼吸を交はします。茶碗もまた使ふ前から水にしめしておいて、潤ひを帯びさせるのが、茶のたしなみとされてゐます。池坊専応は「野山水辺をおのづからなる姿」（口伝）を、自分の流派の新しい花の心として、破れた花器、枯れた枝にも「花」があり、そこに花によるさとりがあるとしました。「古人、皆、花を生けて、悟道したるなり。」禅の影響による、日本の

美の心の目ざめでもあります。　日本の長い内乱の荒廃のなかに生き

た人の心でもありませう。

日本の最も古い歌物語集、短編小説とも見られる話を多く含む

『伊勢物語』（十世紀に成立）のなかに、

なさけある人にて、かめのなかにあやしき藤の花ありけり。花

のしなひ、三尺六寸ばかりなむありける。

といふ、在原行平が客を招くのに花を生けた話があります。花房が

三尺六寸も垂れた藤とは、いかにもあやしく、ほんたうかと疑ふほど

ですが、私はこの藤の花に平安文化の象徴を感じることがあります。

藤の花は日本風にそして女性的に優雅、垂れて咲いて、そよ風に

もゆらぐ風情は、なよやか、つつましやか、やはらかで、初夏のみどりのなかに見えかくれで、もののあはれに通ふやうですが、その花房が三尺六寸となると、異様な華麗でありませう。唐の文化の吸収がよく日本風に消化されて、およそ千年前に、華麗な平安文化を生み、日本の美を確立しましたのは「あやしき藤の花」が咲いたのに似た、異様な奇蹟とも思はれます。歌では初めての勅撰和歌集の『古今集』（九〇五年）、小説では『伊勢物語』、紫式部(九七〇年ごろ―一〇一七年、最終生存資料)の『源氏物語』、清少納言(九六六年ごろ―一〇ろ―一〇〇二年ごろ)の『枕草子』など、日本の古典文学の至上の名作が現れまして、日本の美の伝統をつくり、八百年間ほどの後代の文学に影響をおよぼすといふよりも、支配したのでありました。

殊に『源氏物語』は古今を通じて、日本の最高の小説で、現代にもこれに及ぶ小説はまだなく、十世紀に、このやうに近代的でもある長編小説が書かれたのは、世界の奇蹟として、海外にも広く知られてゐます。少年の私が古語をよく分らぬながら読みましたのも、この平安文学の古典が多く、なかでも『源氏物語』が心におのづからしみこんでゐると思ひます。『源氏物語』の後、日本の小説はこの名作へのあこがれ、そして真似や作り変へが、幾百年も続いたのでありました。和歌は勿論、美術工芸から造園にまで『源氏物語』は深く広く、美の糧となり続けたのであります。

紫式部や清少納言、また和泉式部（九七九年—不明）や赤染衛門*

（およそ九五七年—一〇四一年）などの名歌人もみな宮仕への女性でし

た。平安文化一般が宮廷のそれであり、女性的であるわけです。『源氏物語』や『枕草子』の時は、この文化の最盛期、つまり爛熟の絶頂から頽廃に傾きかける時で、すでに栄華極まった果ての哀愁がただよってゐますが、日本の王朝文化の満開がここに見られます。

やがて王朝は弱まって政権も公卿（くげ）から武士に移って、鎌倉時代（一一九二年―一三三三年）となり、武家の政治が明治元年（一八六八年）まで、おほよそ七百年つづきます。しかし、天皇制も王朝文化も滅び去ったわけではなく、鎌倉初期の勅撰和歌集『新古今集』（一二〇五年）は、平安の『古今集』の技巧的な歌法をさらに進めて、言葉遊びの弊もありますが、妖艶・幽玄・余情を重んじ、感覚の幻想を加へ、近代的な象徴詩に通ふのであります。西行法師（一

一一八年——一一九〇年）は、この二つの時代、平安と鎌倉とをつなぐ

代表的歌人でした。

　　思ひつつ寝ればや人の見えつらむ

　　夢と知りせば覚めざらましを

　　夢路には足を休めず通へども

　　現に一目見しごとはあらず

など『古今集』の小野小町の歌は、夢の歌でもまだ率直に現実的で

すが、それから『新古今集』を経たのち、さらに微妙となった写生、

　　群雀聲する竹にうつる日の

影こそ秋の色になりぬれ

　真萩散る庭の秋風身にしみて

　夕日の影ぞ壁に消えゆく

など、鎌倉末の永福門院＊（一二七一年──一三四二年）のお歌は、日本の繊細な哀愁の象徴で、私により多く近いと感じられます。

「冬雪さえて冷しかりけり」の歌の道元禅師や、「われにともなふ冬の月」の歌の明恵上人は、ほぼ『新古今集』の時代の人でした。

明恵は西行と歌の贈答をし、歌物語もしてゐます。

　西行法師常に来りて物語りして言はく、我が歌を読むは遙かに尋常に異なり。花、ほととぎす、月、雪、すべて万物の興に向

ひても、およそあらゆる相これ虚妄なること、眼に遮り、耳に満てり。また読み出すところの言句は皆これ真言にあらずや。花を読むとも実に花と思ふことなく、月を詠ずれども実に月とも思はず。ただこの如くして、縁に随い、興に随い、読みおくところなり。紅虹たなびけば虚空色どれるに似たり。白日かがやけば虚空明かなるに似たり。しかれども、虚空は本明らかなるものにあらず。また、色どれるにもあらず。我またこの虚空の如くなる心の上において、種々の風情を色どるといへども更に蹤跡なし。この歌即ち是れ如来の真の形体なり。

（弟子喜海の『明恵伝』より）

日本、あるひは東洋の「虚空」、無はここにも言ひあてられてゐ

ます。私の作品を虚無と言ふ評家がありますが、西洋流のニヒリズムといふ言葉はあてはまりません。心の根本がちがふと思ってゐます。道元の四季の歌も「本来ノ面目」と題されてをりますが、四季の美を歌ひながら、実は強く禅に通じたものでせう。

編集注記

道元

鎌倉初期の僧。日本曹洞宗の開祖。内大臣久我通親の子。母は藤原基房の女。母の死などが動機となって無常観から十三歳で出家した。二十四歳で宋に渡り、如浄禅師に曹洞禅を学び帰国。永平寺を建立。道元は、悟りを得るために座禅をするのではなく、座禅そのものが悟りであると説いて「人とは何か」「いかに生くべきか」を探求しつづけた。著書に、『正法眼蔵』のほか『学道用心集』『普勧坐禅儀』などがある。

明恵上人

鎌倉初期の華厳宗の僧。名は高辮。八歳で父母と死別して九歳で出家し、高尾山や東大寺で、密教や華厳をおさめた。後鳥羽上皇・北条泰時らにその学徳を慕われ、秀れた僧としてきこえた。著書に『摧邪輪』など七十余書がある。

西行法師（一一一八—一一九〇年）

平安末から鎌倉初期の歌人。藤原秀郷から九代目の子孫にあたり、鳥羽院の北面の武士であったが、二十三歳のとき、出家。以後諸国を放浪し自然を詠む。自然を愛し自然を生きた歌人として、幽玄の境地を拓いた。歌集に『山家集』『西行上人歌集』などがあり、二千百余首の歌がある。

末期の眼

芥川龍之介・梶井基次郎・竹久夢二などの死に触れて、芸術家の「業」に肉迫した。昭和八年に発表した川端氏のエッセー。

維摩居士

大乗仏教の一経典「維摩経」の中で、中心となって活躍する居士の名。その中で、実は、菩薩の化身であると説かれ、いわば大乗仏教の理想的人間像として描かれた在家の信者。

金冬心（一六八七—一七六三年）

中国清代の書家・画家・詩人。"冬心"と号し、詩人として出発したが、中年から絵をかきはじめた。竹・山水・仏像などの絵を南宋画の名家に学んだが、その形式主義のわくを破って新鮮で個性的な表現をした。著書に『冬心集』がある。

千利休（一五二二—一五九一年）

安土桃山時代の茶匠。信長・秀吉に「茶道者」として仕え、茶道理論の大成者として知られる。

赤染衛門

平安中期の女流歌人。衛門の名は、父赤染時用が右衛門尉だったことによる。藤原道長の妻倫子・中宮彰子に仕え和泉式部と並び称せられた。三十六歌仙の一人。歌集に『赤染衛門集』があり、『栄華物語』の作者ともいわれる。